The Female Pope

by Oliver Hayes

Publisher
Website - www.BretwaldaBooks.com
Twitter - @Bretwaldabooks
Facebook - Bretwalda Books
Blog - bretwaldabooks.blogspot.co.uk/

First Published 2017
Text Copyright © Oliver Hayes 2017
Photos and illustrations Copyright © Oliver Hayes 2017, unless otherwise stated
Rupert Matthews asserts his moral rights to be regarded as the author of this work.

Acknowledgements

Photos, illustrations and maps are from the author's collection except:

Contents

FOREWORD

For many centuries it was accepted almost without discussion that the priesthood, and pastoral work more generally, was exclusively a male domain. Women had a role within the Christian Church, as nuns or lay workers, but the giving of the sacraments was seen as a male preserve. Recently this view has been questioned. Some scholars have pointed to accounts of the Early Church that indicate women had some sort of a role in the staffing of the Church. Some denominations have recently allowed the ordination of women: the Anglicans from 1992, the United Church of Canada since 1936 and Methodism since it was founded in the 18th century.

The Roman Catholic Church has, by contrast, stood firm against the ordination of women. The issue began to be raised in the 1970s, and more seriously in the 1980s Pope John Paul II issued the apostolic letter "Ordinatio sacerdotalis" in May 1994. In it he stated " the Church has no authority whatsoever to confer priestly ordination on women and that this judgment is to be definitively held by all the Church's faithful." Canon law No.1024 is equally clear "Only a baptised man can validly receive sacred ordination."

It would seem clear, therefore, that Catholic priests must be male. By extension those higher up the ladder of authority within the Church must be male too for only priests may be bishops, archbishops, cardinals or, indeed, pope. And yet for centuries rumours and legends have swirled about that one woman did get to be pope in Rome. The Catholic Church has always denied the stories, but they refuse to go away.

It is now time to look anew at these old stories and try to discover the truth that lies behind them.

Chapter 1
The Legend of the Female Pope

The legend of the female pope comes in many forms and details vary considerably. However, as the tale is usually recounted it goes something like this.

Soon after the year 800 a girl named Joan was born into the Anglicus family of minor nobility at Mainz, Germany. Her parents being somewhat indulgent, the girl was allowed to study books as well as the more customary skills needed to run a household and bring up a family. She showed such talent for learning that she was permitted to acquire a small library and to

Below: Mainz Cathedral. The current building was begun in 991 and so Joan would have studied at the predecessor that was demolished to make way for this structure.

Above: The Parthenon in Athens. Built to be a temple to the goddess Athena, by the time Joan came here it was a church dedicated to the Virgin Mary.

attend lectures in theology and philosophy at the school attached to Mainz Cathedral. Fearing a minor scandal, and wary of their daughter's safety wandering about alone, Joan's family insisted that she dress as a boy and call herself "John".

As "John Anglicus" progressed through his teenage years her precocious talents were noticed and remarked upon. At some point "John's" parents died and she was free to continue her academic career in the guise of a man. In the 9th century such a career was generally open only to a monk or member of the clergy. Living cost money, and books were formidably expensive before the invention of printing lowered the cost massively. Only a rich person, or one supported by the Church, could hope to avoid the need to work for a living. "John" therefore entered the Church in order to continue with the academic work she loved so much.

"John" then moved to study in Athens, then a part of the Byzantine Empire. Everyone in Greece accepted "John" as a scholar from Germany. There was, however, one man who knew the truth. Either in Athens or just before she left Germany, "John" met and fell in love with a fellow scholar. She revealed her true sex to the man and the two became discrete lovers.

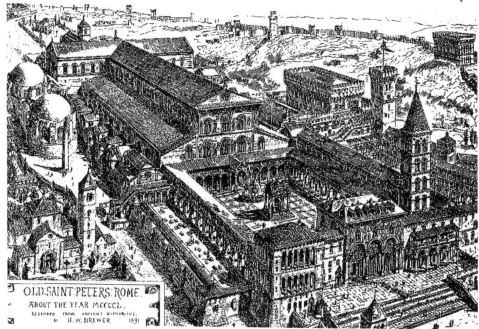

Abvoe: The old St Peter's Basilica in Rome. This structure was begun by the Roman Emperor Constantine in 318 to serve as the main church for the Christians of Rome. It survived over a thousand years until it was demolished in the 15th century to be replaced by the current St Peter's.

Having learned all she could from the Byzantines, "John" moved to Rome where the greatest libraries of western Christendom were to be found. Her growing reputation as a scholar led to "John" being in demand as a lecturer and preacher. Her talks became famous for their erudition and humanity, attracting large and distinguished audiences.

When the reigning pope died, the clergy and people of Rome gathered to elect a successor. They unanimously chose "John Anglicus" to be the Bishop of Rome, and so the next pope. "Pope John" moved into the Lateran Palace and took up the reins of power. At first all went well, but after a short reign as pope, "John" fell pregnant. This rather inconvenient fact was covered up successfully as the pope pretended to be ill, but eventually "John" was forced to attend a service in St Peter's Basilica. As "Pope John" was riding in procession from the Lateran to St Peter's she passed down Via di San Gi   anni.

8

Suddenly the Pope collapsed off her horse in pain. She suffered a late miscarriage, losing blood heavily and contracted an infection from the dirty street. Fever set in and within days she was dead. She had been pope for two years, seven months and four days.

The Catholic Church was horrified by the scandal. Those who had seen the pope collapse were bribed or intimidated into silence. The reign of Pope John was consigned to the past and the Church moved on to a new era under a new pope. A small statue of an anonymous woman was erected in the Via di San Giovanni, then it was neglected. The fact that a woman had once sat on the throne of St Peter was forgotten.

But, of course, such an important secret could not be kept hidden for ever. People who had been sworn to secrecy told their children about the day that they had seen a pope give birth. The official records may have been purged, but enough of the truth remained for later historians to notice discrepancies. For instance Pope John's immediate successors, who were in on the secret, never went down the Via di San Giovanni. And once that tradition was established later popes avoided the street, though they did not know why. The truth lived on in legends, rumours and misremembered facts.

Below: Pope Joan giving birth during a procession in Rome. Engraving from Giovanni Boccacio's 14th cnetury De Claris Mulieribus, which retold the story of Pope Joan in great detail.

Left: Martin of Troppau. From the middle of the 13th century, Martin was active in Rome as confessor and chaplain for Pope Alexander IV and his successors, Pope Urban IV, Pope Clement IV, Pope Gregory, Pope Innocent V, Pope Adrian V and Pope John XXI (d. 1277), the last pope to appear in his chronicles. On 22 June 1278, Pope Nicholas III, while in Viterbo, appointed him Archbishop of Gniezno. His access to the papal archives give his works great credibility.

The legend first got into writing in about 1240 when the Dominican friar Jean de Mailly wrote his "Universal Chronicle of Metz". He mentioned the story in passing, dating it to immediately after the reign of Pope Victor III, who died in 1087.

According to Mailly, "John" had worked in the curia before being elected pope. When she was discovered, the mob pounced on her and stoned her to death in utter disgust at the deception she had practised on them. A rather fuller version of the legend was included in the writings of the French monk Stephen de Bourbon at about the same time.

In the 1260s an anonymous chronicle written in Erfurt expanded the tale and included many of the details that flesh out the bare story told by Mailly. However it was the Dominian historian Martin of Troppau who gave the fullest early version of the story in his "Chronicle of Popes and Emperors" in the 1280s.

The legend was broadly believed and accepted across Europe from the time of Martin of Troppau until the 16th century, when the Catholic Church began to deny it vehemently. Indeed when the cathedral of Siena was being built the architects included a marble bust of every pope from St Peter to the date of building - and Pope Joan was among them.

A key weakness of the story was that it did not get into writing until some three centuries after it was supposed to have happened. Such a gap in the written record is traditionally held to cast doubt on any story.

However, by the very nature of a scandalous story apparently hushed up at the time, the tale of the female pope would not have been written down at the time, at least not in any form likely to see the light of day.

So what truth was there, if any, behind the legend of a female pontiff?

Below: Sienna Cathedral. The horizontal moulding around the nave and the presbytery contains 172 plaster busts of popes dating from the 15th and 16th centuries starting with St. Peter and ending with Lucius III. Pope Joan is featured prominently.

Chapter 2
The Legend under Scrutiny

Just because a story does not get written down until many years after it is supposed to have taken place does not mean that it is untrue. "Absence of evidence does not mean evidence of absence" as the old historian's saying has it.

In ascertaining whether there was any truth behind the legend it is necessary to evaluate the sources for it and to see if the details of the story are credible in any meaningful way.

The main source for the story is Martin of Troppau, and on the face of it he was a man who should have known what he was writing about. Martin was born in Troppau (now Opava). When he was born there the town was in the Margraviate of Moravia, a part of the Holy Roman Empire.

Left: The coat of arms of the Orsini family. The Orsini family is an Italian noble family; it was one of the most influential princely families in medieval Italy and renaissance Rome. Members of the Orsini include popes Celestine III (1191–1198), Nicholas III (1277–1280), and Benedict XIII (1724–1730), 34 cardinals and numerous condottieri and other significant political and religious figures.

It is now in the Czech Republic, and Martin himself came from a Polish family. As a young man, Martin joined the Dominican Order and was ordained a priest.

In about 1250, Martin moved to Rome. Sometime around 1255 he became the private chaplain to Pope Alexander IV, and soon afterwards his confessor. Martin remained papal confessor and chaplain to the popes Pope Urban IV, Pope Clement IV, Pope Gregory, Pope Innocent V, Pope Adrian V and Pope John XXI. The next pope, Nicholas III, for some reason did not want Martin's services and sent him to be Archbishop of Gnienzo in Poland. Martin never got there. He reached only so far as Bologna before he fell suddenly ill and died within hours. He was buried in the Basilica of St Dominic. There have been rumours that he had been poisoned.

While no guilty person was named in any of the rumours that got into writing, it does not take much imagination to see a finger pointing at Nicholas III, or somebody close to him. Before becoming pope, Nicholas had been known as Giovanni Orsini, a scion of one of the richest, most powerful - and most ruthless - families of noblemen in central Italy. Nicholas himself was notoriously corrupt. He made four members of his family cardinals, gave well-paid and influential jobs in the Church to many others and was accused of having bribed his way into the papacy.

As former papal confessor, Martin of Troppau knew a lot of secrets. The Orsini family had a lot to lose and may well have wanted to ensure Martin's silence - permanently.

It is therefore clear that Martin had access to the innermost secrets of the papacy. If there had been a female pope, Martin would very likely have found out about it. So many years after the event he may have thought that there was no harm in writing about it. Perhaps the Orsini thought otherwise. Unlike Martin's ancestors, the Orsini family had been active and important in Rome at the time the female pope was supposed to have held power. Perhaps they had played a role in her rise to power, or in her government, and wanted to keep those details secret.

Given that the main source for the story of a female pope is credible, attention must then turn to whether the story itself is at all likely.

Europe in the 9th century was undoubtedly a man's world. It was a tough place where families had to resort to arms to hang on to their lands and estates. Vikings roamed the northern waters, pillaging and killing whenever they got the chance. In the east the pagan Magyars raided and slaughtered wherever their horses could take them. Even in the supposedly more civilised and secure lands around the Mediterranean there were plenty of tough, unscrupulous men willing to use swords and bloodshed to take what they wanted. It was no place for a woman to set up on her own unless she had tough brothers willing to do the violent work for her.

Nor were women really expected to do much in public life. Most women spent a much larger proportion of their lives either pregnant or breast feeding than is the norm now. Running a business or handling large estates involved long hours on horseback in rain and wind, not something that a pregnant woman would risk given the poor medical standards of the day. Instead women ran the households and did the accounts while the men went out to get wet, sleep in the open and get involved in fights.

If a woman wanted to pursue a career in business, politics or the Church she had to avoid becoming frequently pregnant, and that meant not getting married. In that day and age this alone would be unusual for anyone, but for a young woman from a good family it was almost unheard of. Entering a convent was a possibility, but nuns were expected to stay put in their convent and lead a cloistered life. Clearly Joan Anglicus was more adventurous than that with a greater appetite for learning. And, as we have also seen, she was not entirely adverse to the company of men.

So having begun dressing as a boy for safety reasons, Joan will have found it useful to have continued to dress as a man. Unless her female figure was too obvious she could, clad in a loose robe, have passed for a fresh-faced youth. If she moved on every few years, as she seems to have done, and re-announced herself as being 18 years old each time she arrived in a new town she could have kept up the pretence for some years. Having another monk in tow, her lover as it seems, would have helped the pretence for she would have arrived with somebody to vouch for her, or him.

But early medieval Europe was not really a place with much privacy. Families slept together in single-roomed cottages, knights slept in great halls surrounded by their men-at-arms and monks slept in communal dormitaries. Monastic toilets were usually rooms with half a dozen seats with no partitions. Nudity when bathing, again communally, was the norm. In such circumstances is it really possible that a woman could conceal her true sex when all around her were men?

Such a feat seems to strain credulity, and yet historical records show that many women managed to achieve it. In August 1862 the 95th Illinois Infantry took on a batch of recruits, one of whom gave his name as Albert Cashier. The regiment marched off to fight in the American Civil War, taking part in the Siege of Vicksburg, the Battle of Guntown and the Red River Campaign among other actions. Contemporary records state Cashier to be "slight" and "short", but otherwise he did not attract any undue attention. Cashier was, in fact, Jennie Hodgers. She maintained her pretence of being a man until wounded when a medical attendant discovered the truth. Hodgers later readopted the name of Cashier and dressed as a man, keeping constantly on the move perhaps to avoid anyone getting to know her too well.

Rather more successful in concealing her sex was Hannah Snell. In 1746 her husband ran off with all their money, so Snell borrowed a suit of male

Left: Hannah Snell. In 1747 Snell joined the Royal Marines of the British navy. She fought in several campaigns without anyone suspecting that she was really a woman. After she retired from the armed services she published her story and went on the stage before opening a pub which she named "The Female Warrior".

clothes from her sister's husband and set off to track her husband down. She eventually found him, but by then he was dead having been executed for murder. Penniless, miles from home and with no living family she was approached by a recruiting sergeant from the Royal Marines and signed up. In 1747 her ship, HMS Swallow, left Britain for India. In 1748 she took part in the attack on a French fortress at Pondicherry and in other actions before her ship returned in 1750. As the ship was being paid off, Snell revealed her true sex to her shipmates - apparently to their utter astonishment. The event made her a celebrity. She sold her story to the press and went on the stage - always playing parts that involved her dressing as a man for at least part of the play. She remarried and had two children.

A closer parallel to Joan Anglicus might be "James Barry". This Barry graduated from Edinburgh University as a surgeon in 1813. After working in a local hospital he joined the British army as a hospital assistant. Having served his apprenticeship he became an army surgeon and was sent out to Belgium to take part in the bloody Waterloo campaign in which he distinguished himself. Working his way up through the ranks of the army medical corps, Barry served in Canada, the West Indies, South Africa and Malta. Eventually he reached the rank of Inspector General of Military Hospitals and retired laden with honours and accolades in 1864. Barry died of dysentery in 1865, and it was only as his body was being washed for burial was it discovered that "James" was a woman.

Subsequent research sought to track Barry's career back to find out who she had really been. The University of Edinburgh was the obvious place to start. The officials there maintained stoutly that they had believed their pupil to be a young man. All they knew was the "James Barry" had arrived from Ireland in 1809 with plenty of money and a letter of introduction from a highly respected Dublin solicitor. That solicitor was long dead, of course, but his files remained. One of those was labelled "James Barry". It contained only one sheet of paper, an instruction stating that any letters or official correspondence to or about James Barry should be forwarded to a Mrs Mary-Ann Bulkley. Mrs Bulkley was also dead, but family members did have some information. They recalled a daughter named Margaret Ann who had left Ireland to go to train as a nurse somewhere on mainland Britain.

It would appear, therefore, that Margaret Ann Bulkley left Ireland at the age of about 20 to train as a nurse but that when she arrived in Scotland she

Right: Dr James Barry (left) with John, a servant, and his dog Psyche, c. 1862, Jamaica. James Miranda Stuart Barry (c. 1789-1799 – 25 July 1865, born Margaret Ann Bulkley), was an Irish military surgeon in the British Army. He chose to live as a man so that he might be accepted as a university student and able to pursue a career as a surgeon, with his sex only being discovered by the public and his colleagues after his death. Barry was the first qualified female British doctor or surgeon known, anticipating Elizabeth Garrett Anderson by over 50 years.

dressed as a man in order to train as a doctor instead. She kept up the pretence of being a male throughout the next 56 years. Of course, "James Barry" had the advantage that, as a surgeon and an officer, she would have had more privacy than a common soldier. But on campaign even senior officers would find themselves sharing beds, tents and washing facilities. If Barry could keep up the pretence for so long, Joan Anglicus must have been able to do so as well.

It seems, therefore, that it is possible for a woman to adopt and maintain the disguise of a man even in conditions - such as on board a cramped warship or on campaign - when this might seem to be impossible. Joan Anglicus would no doubt have had to work hard at the deception but it was possible.

Turning next to her alleged career as a scholar there are some interesting things to note. She is said to have started her education in Mainz, at the cathedral school. At this date the Catholic Church maintained schools at every cathedral for the education of those young men wishing to enter the priesthood or become monks. Most of these schools allowed other youngsters to attend the classes even if they had no intention of a Church career so long as their families paid a fee. The aim was to educate the next generation of noblemen and merchants both to respect the Church and to provide them with an appreciation of the finer things in life and tempt them away from hunting, fighting and chasing women.

It is therefore entirely reasonable for a child from a minor noble family, such as the Anglicus, to attend a cathedral school. It was usual for girls, if they were to be educated at all, to be taught at home by a tutor but a few are known to have attended school before they reached a marriageable age. Young Joan may well have been sent to school by her family, and adopting the clothes of a boy would have helped her to avoid attention, certainly once she got past the age of ten or so.

The problem is, however, that the church at Mainz was not raised to the dignity of being a cathedral until 911. Joan must have been going to school about a century earlier than that. Some have alleged that Mainz did not have a school then, but this is by no means certain. Many monasteries and churches maintained schools even though they were not obliged to do so, as were cathedrals. It may be that Joan was educated at Mainz and that later writers who were living at a time when the Mainz Cathedral School was a well known centre of learning just assumed that she must have attended that school.

Not all of Joan's movements are known, but the stay in Athens is well recorded. This was an interesting choice. At the time the accepted places to go and get a good education were Rome, Constantinople, Milan and Bologna. By the time historians were writing about Joan Bologna was the leading university in the West, with Paris not far behind. And yet they agree that she went to study in Athens, which in their day was a run down town of no real importance. But in the early 9th century Athens had been different. Athens had shrunk considerably since its glory days in Classical antiquity, but it was still a sizeable and prosperous city and a centre of learning. The Parthenon, once the Temple of Athene, was by this date a Christian church. There were also several monasteries in and around Athens which harboured records of ancient, rare texts. These were mostly written in Greek, then a language not widely understood in the West. If Joan wanted to learn about the writings of Plato, Aristotle and other ancient authors she would have needed to go to the Byzantine Empire. The capital, Constantinople, might have seemed a more obvious place to go, but there were problems.

At this date the western and eastern branches of Christianity were in serious conflict. The Patriarch of Constantinople had excommunicated the

Pope, who returned the favour. There were doctrinal differences at issue in this dispute, including the bitter Filoque Controversy. This centred around whether the Holy Spirit was equal to Jesus (as the Byzantines believed) or subservient to him (as the Popes taught). But there were serious political issues as well.

The Byzantine Empire was ruled by Emperors who could trace an unbroken line of succession back to the ancient Roman Empire. Indeed, although they were Christians and spoke Greek, the Byzantines believed that they were the sole inheritors of the Roman tradition and legal right to rule.

Below: The coronation of Charlemagne as Holy Roman Emperor in 800, as shown in a 19th century painting by Friedrich Kaulbach. Charlemagne's coronation as Emperor, though intended to represent the continuation of the unbroken line of Emperors from Augustus to Constantine VI, had the effect of setting up two separate (and often opposing) Empires and two separate claims to imperial authority. For centuries to come, the Emperors of both West and East would make competing claims of sovereignty.

They claimed, in theory if not in fact, that the entire old Roman Empire belonged to them. Italy, France, Britain, Spain and North Africa may have been overrun by barbarians, but the legal right to rule them resided in Constantinople.

The old western half of the Roman Empire had collapsed in the 5th century. In ad476 the last Emperor in Rome, Romulus Augustulus, had been forced to abdicate by the German king Odoacer, who was eager to rule Italy in his place. Odoacer sent the imperial regalia to the Emperor in Constantinople with flowery phrases about how the Italians no longer needed their own emperor and would like the Eastern Emperor to take over, just so long as he did not actually interfere in how Odoacer ran the place. The Byzantines had made periodic efforts to reconquer Italy, but other than getting a toe hold on Sicily and Calabria had never achieved much.

Then on Christmas Day 800 Pope Leo III had crowned King Charles of the Franks to be "Emperor of Rome". The act was a political move. Charles, better known to history as Charlemagne, ruled most of western Europe, about half of the old western Empire. The papacy, meanwhile, needed protection from Moslem raiders from North Africa. Charlemagne gave the military protection and got an impressive title in return.

The Byzantines, however, were furious. They viewed Charlemagne as a jumped up barbarian usurper with no right to use the title of Emperor and the legal right to rule that it implied. The diplomatic row rumbled on for centuries and was never really resolved before the Byzantine Empire finally fell to the Moslem Turks in 1453.

At the time "John Anglicus" wanted to go to the east to study Greek learning both the theological and political disputes were running very high indeed. Constantinople would not have been a welcoming place for a western monk to go. The authorities would have watched her actions carefully and, for obvious reasons, this was something "John" wanted to avoid. Athens may not have had such magnificent libraries and teachers as Constantinople, but it was better than nothing and the chances of escaping attention would have been much higher. It is therefore exactly the place to which "John" would have gone.

But there is another interesting fact about Athens in the first half of the 9th century. In 752 a woman named Irene Sarantapechaina had been born in Athens. Like Joan Anglicus, Irene was born into a minor noble family of no great importance. Like Joan she proved to be an exceptionally fine scholar as a child and was given a top quality education in Athens. Unlike Joan, Irene did not hide her female sex. Indeed, she and her family celebrated and boasted of her learning and intellectual gifts. It was for this reason that in November 769 she was sent to Constantinople. The then Emperor Constantine VI was looking for a suitable bride for his son, Leo. As was usual among Byzantine nobility at the time this process involved what was known as a "Bride Show".

A Bride Show took place when a nobleman let it be known that he was looking for a bride either for himself or for a member of his family. Other noble families who thought that they had a suitable bride then sent the girl, together with servants and chaperone, to the household of the nobleman to be tested for suitability. Of course, every nobleman had his own idea about what would make a good bride. Constantine seems to have wanted a girl for Leo who was a similar age, well educated, intelligent but not from one of the great noble families. Choosing a bride from one of the important families would only cause trouble with the others. Irene was perfect. Leo was 19, while she was 17, she was obviously well educated and clever and came from a suitably obscure family from the provinces. She married Leo 6 weeks after arriving in Constantinople. When Leo became Emperor, she became empress and when Leo died young she ruled the Byzantine Empire as regent for her son.

The career of Irene Sarantapechaina was well known. Perhaps Joan was drawn to Athens because of Irene's career. Even if her true sex were to be unmasked, the Athenians did not seem to have any qualms about women scholars. Joan's thirst for learning could be assuaged in Athens in safety. In the event, of course, her pretence continued.

Joan is next recorded as having gone to Rome. Her age at this point is unclear, but she must have been in her late 20s or early 30s. It was a natural next move for her. "All roads lead to Rome" was a common medieval saying indicating that whatever path a scholar or churchman took in life his career path would eventually take him to Rome. That city was the centre of the Catholic Church, so whether a man chose to be a monk, priest, preacher, lawyer or doctor he would, if he rose high enough in his profession, end up in Rome.

And so "John Anglicus" went to Rome as she climbed ever higher in her career as a scholar. Her activities in Rome ring true. She read, studied and gave lectures. This is exactly what a leading scholar was expected to do in the first half of the 9th century. Learning was important in its own right, but it was also important to pass on that learning to others.

Moreover at this date there was little in the way of formal higher education. Once a person left school being able to read, write, add up and with a basic knowledge of the scriptures things became much less formal. A lecturer, such as Joan became in Rome, taught whoever turned up to lectures. There was no formal body of students nor a set curriculum. Anyone could stroll into a lecture. It was for this reason that high Church officials could attend Joan's talks. The subject and speaker would be advertised in advance, then whoever was interested would come along. Of course there was pressure on speakers to put forward interesting material and to be great performers and orators. Any one who spoke in a monotone about dull subjects would soon find themselves addressing empty halls. Joan, it must be assumed, was a stirring speaker and original thinker.

And in many ways the line between a lecturer and preacher was blurred. At a time when nearly all learning involved either theology or law, and frequently both, any teacher would find themselves preaching. Again, this would attract clergy of all levels. And if "John" were putting forward interesting aspects of theology the talks would become much talked about, and so increase "John's" reputation.

That a scholar from outside Rome could build up a following of rich and influential people is perfectly reasonable. Rome had a constantly shifting population at this time, especially among the clergy. Men would come to Rome for a short visit on Church business, or take up appointments lasting a year or two, then return to their native lands or perhaps be sent off on a mission somewhere quite exotic. A foreign preacher would be nothing new.

Nor would there be any language barrier. Every churchman learned Latin at a young age. All books were written in Latin. Originally this was because Latin had been the mother tongue of the Roman Empire, but since the fall of Rome the tradition was maintained because it meant all literate people could read the same books no matter what their mother tongue. And given how extremely expensive books were in the days before printing, it meant that precious books and the learning they contained could move easily across Europe.

The native population of cooks, tailors, cobblers and servants that made up the bulk of the Roman population earned a good living from the Churchmen who came and went. To them Joan was, no doubt, just another ambitious foreigner come to try their luck in the great city.

The account of Joan's election to the papacy is at first sight very odd. It is said that the clergy and people of Rome met and elected "John" to be the next pope. Today papal elections are conducted in quite different fashion. When a pope dies or abdicates, cardinals gather from all over the world to meet in a secretive conclave in the Sistine Chapel. Those cardinals are the leading Catholic churchmen of their country, so all the Christian nations are represented and get a voice in choosing the Pope. Once in the conclave, the cardinals are shut off from the world, they vote in successive secret ballots until one cardinal gains a two-thirds majority. The winner is then announced to the waiting crowds.

But back in the 9th century elections were very different. Take the cardinals for a start. Today's cardinals may come from all over the world, but officially they are the parish priests and deacons of Rome. Each cardinal is nominally attached to one of the parishes of the city, though of course they do not actually officiate or carry out duties there. Over the centuries it has become the practice for the Church to reward service and dedication among senior clergy by making them a clergyman of Rome. Thus the cardinals are, in theory at least, the clergy of Rome.

The people of Rome are, however, another matter. These days the people of Rome get no voice at all in the election of Pope, nor did they at the time that the story of Pope Joan was being written down. In the 9th century they did. The very earliest popes had been elected by all the Christians of the city. The election seems to have been held in a field outside the city walls, with the voting being done by show of hands. As paganism waned and the entire population of the city became Christian this was no longer feasible. Instead a process evolved by which the clergy of Rome selected candidates who then sought support from the richer, more noble and more influential citizens. Usually it soon became clear which person was going to be most acceptable to the clergy and the leading citizens. If there was no obviously leading candidate some sort of election would then take place. We are not entirely certain what form this took, but it seems to have involved a mass meeting near the Lateran Palace at which there was a good deal of shouting, shoving and general mayhem.

The facade of the Lateran Basilica, added to the old church some centuries after the time of the female pope.

Nor was it necessary for a person to be a cardinal before they could be elected Pope. Any Christian was eligible. It was not even necessary in the 9th century for the person to be a priest. Anyone could be elected.

On the face of it, therefore, John Anglicus might have been elected. As a leading preacher and respected theologian who was popular with the crowd, respected by the clergy and supported by the richer citizens, he would be just the sort of person to be elected Pope. Having got this far with a successful deception, Joan may have reasoned that she might as well accept the nomination and become Pope. Why not?

If this is what happened it might make sense of what happened next. To have reached this exalted position would have taken a good number of years. Joan would no longer have been a young woman. She would have been at an age when her fertility was declining. Perhaps she and her secret monk-lover grew careless, and so she became pregnant - with fatal consequences.

Unfortunately it is at the step of her election to the papacy that the credibility of the story breaks down. That a woman masquerading as a man could have evaded discovery for years is quite believable. That she could rise high in the world of scholarship is credible. That having done so she would have moved to Rome and mixed with the great and the good is highly probable. But that an outsider from north of the Alps would be elected pope in the mid-9th century was quite impossible.

The papacy at this date was in a state of flux. For centuries the primary duty of the pope had been his role as Bishop of Rome. Like any bishop he spent most of his time ministering to his flock. Although the Bishop of Rome

Facing page: The facade of the Lateran Basilica, added to the old church some centuries after the time of the female pope. The Papal Archbasilica of St. John in Lateran (Italian: Arcibasilica Papale di San Giovanni in Laterano), commonly known as St. John Lateran Archbasilica, St. John Lateran Basilica, St. John Lateran, or simply the Lateran Basilica, is the cathedral church of Rome, Italy and therefore houses the cathedra, or ecclesiastical seat, of the Roman Pontiff (Pope). It is the oldest of and has precedence among the four papal major basilicas, all of which are in Rome, because it is the oldest church in the West and houses the cathedra of the Roman Pontiff. It has the title of ecumenical mother church of the Roman Catholic faithful.

had long been recognised as the successor to St Peter, the rock on which Christ promised to build his Church and the first Bishop of Rome, this gave the pope no real power. He was listened to with respect in theological debates and was reckoned to be one of the most senior figures in the Church. But no pope claimed to be head of the Catholic Church in the way that popes would become later in the middle ages and remain to this day. And the Romans liked to have a Roman as their bishop.

Another factor that was in play at this date was that of the nobles. Until the later 8th century the popes, like all bishops, had been reliant on bequests, legacies and land to provide an income. The Bishop of Rome was always rather richer than other bishops, but not dramatically so. However, the popes had recently been granted the Papal States as feudal states to rule over, tax and govern. This made the pope not just a bishop but also a secular prince. The aim had been to secure for the papacy a good, steady income from taxation along with a reserve of men to be mobilised for war should the Moslem raiders return.

The popes had imagined that having acquired extensive and prosperous cities and states in central Italy they would be able to govern them in much the same way they had previously governed the Church. The local nobles did not like that at all. In other states, even those ruled by the most autocratic of kings, the nobles had some say in the government. The ruler used them as officials, relied on them for taxation and put them in command of armies. Even a king cannot be everywhere at once. But the popes behaved differently. They staffed their government with clerics from other countries, drew a nice income from other dioceses and hired mercenaries to fight their wars. The local nobles were frozen out and resented it.

To get some grip on the government of the state they lived in the nobles took to manipulating papal elections to their own benefit. The wanted one of their own to be pope and, by and large, that is what they got. A quick look at the popes elected in the early 9th century and the social position of their father's makes the point.

Stephen IV - elected 816 - Roman aristocrat
Paschal I - elected 817 - Roman merchant
Eugene II - elected 824 - Roman
Valentine - elected 827 - Roman aristocrat
Gregory IV - elected 827 - Roman aristocrat

Sergius II - elected 844 - Roman aristocrat
Leo IV - elected 847 - Milanese soldier resident in Rome
The second half of the century is not much different.

The ways in which the nobility ensured that their favoured candidate got elected varied considerably. In 816 they did not have to do much, Stephen being a hugely popular deacon. In 817 they spread rumours that an army of Franks was being sent by Emperor Louis to force a German barbarian into office, ensuring that the electors quickly installed Pashal into office. In 824

The apse of the Lateran Basilica with, at its centre, the papal throne. Pope Sylvester I presided over the official dedication of the archbasilica and the adjacent Lateran Palace in 324, declaring both to be a "Domus Dei" ("House of God"). The papal cathedra was placed in its interior, rendering it the cathedral of the Pope qua Bishop of Rome.

it looked as if the people might endorse a famously holy but slightly unworldly priest being put forward by the clergy. The nobility then sent in gangs of toughs to foment trouble, spark riots and beat up opponents. After three months of street fights and bloodshed the clergy backed down and accepted Eugene, the nobles' choice.

The first election of 827 was trouble free, Valentine gaining the support of clergy, nobles and people. The second election that year was dominated by the nobles who put forward Gregory and made threatening noises to a priest who considered putting his name forward.

The election of 844 was considerably more eventful. Within hours of the death of Gregory IV, the people of Rome had backed a deacon named John. A vast mob of citizens poured into the streets, carrying John shoulder high to the Lateran Palace. They surged into the Lateran Basilica and enthroned John in the papal chair. A priest was found to perform the necessary rituals, but the Bishop of Ostia, whose task this properly was, could not be found.

Meanwhile the nobles had been meeting in the Basilica of San Martino to decide who they wanted to put forward as their candidate in the coming election. They had just chosen an elderly aristocratic priest named Sergius when news arrived about the enthronement of John. The nobles promptly sent messengers galloping off to their castles and estates to summon their armed retainers. A couple of days later, the armies of the nobles having arrived, they marched on the Lateran. The doors and windows were barricaded shut, but axes were produced and before long a full blown battle was raging for possession of the Lateran. Eventually the nobles and their men got in, showing no mercy to the men inside who were cut down by swords, axes and anything else that came to hand. John fled, but was caught and trussed up.

Sergius was then led into the Lateran Basilica, blood still running across the floor, and enthroned in his turn. John was dragged forward and thrown at his feet. Sergius ordered him to be confined in a monastery for the rest of his life. He is never heard of again.

After that the election of 847 came as something of an anticlimax. Leo had the support of both clergy and nobility, and the people meekly accepted him.

That a woman could pass herself off as a man in a monastery was clearly possible, that she could rise to have a reputation as a great scholar is likely it might even be ventured that she might conceivably have risen to a position that she might stand a chance of being elected pope. Such things may be unlikely but are not impossible. But that a German would be elected Pope - not a chance.

There is one name in the list of the 9th century that is of interest - that of John the priest who was so violently ejected from the Lateran Basilica in 844. The female pope was supposed to have been using the name of John. It will be recalled that she was said to have collapsed and had a miscarriage in Via di San Giovanni, after which her papacy ended. The Via di San Giovanni lies just a hundred yards from the Lateran. It is possible, though there is no documentary evidence, that as this John fled from the Lateran he was caught

Below: The interior of San Martino ai Monti. San Martino ai Monti (Italian for "St Martin in the Mountains"), officially known as Santi Silvestro e Martino ai Monti ("SS Sylvester & Martin in the Mountains"), is a minor basilica in Rome, Italy, in the Rione Monti neighbourhood. It is located near the edge of the Parque de Monte Oppio, near the corner of Via Equizia and Viale del Monte Oppio, about five to six blocks south of Santa Maria Maggiore.

in that very road.

Although Martin of Troppau states that the female pope John took office after Leo IV and the priest John made his abortive bid for power after the death of Gregory IV there are only 11 years between the two events. It is very possible that Martin, writing in the 13th century, was writing about this John and got the dates muddled.

But if that were the case, was John the Priest a German woman? It would appear not. He is known to have lived in Rome for a good many years and seems to have been a native of the city. Moreover there is no suggestion that he was ever unmasked as being anything other than the elderly, devout male priest that he claimed to be. So while John the Priest might be a good fit for the originator of a legend of a short-lived Pope who fell from power in embarrassing circumstances in the Via di San Giovanni, he does not fit the idea of a female pope.

The question then arises of where such an idea came from. To find the answer we need to look forwards to about 50 years after John the Priest to the time when a quite extraordinary woman was born in Rome: Marozia.

Chapter 3
The Real Female Pope

Marozia was born in Rome in the year 890, her precise date of birth not being recorded. Her family was of the highest in Italy. Her father was Count Theophylact of Tusculum, her mother Countess Theodora, herself of noble Roman parentage. Marozia was thus born into wealthy and comfortable circumstances of which most people of her time could only dream. She received a good education, though like most noble girls she was brought up to marry well and secure useful lands or political contacts for her family.

Her mother's cousin, like many Roman younger sons, entered the Church. This Sergius became Bishop of Portus. This was a massively lucrative sinecure. The town of Portus, at its height, had a population of around 50,000. Its bishop had gained a correspondingly impressive palatial residence and extensive estates to produce rents to pay for the many demands on his purse from the 50,000 souls in his care. But then the branch of the Tiber River that fed the harbour at Portus silted up and the docks became useless. The population left to such an extent that the city became a mere mass of ruins. The Bishop of Portus no longer had souls to care for, nor parishes to visit, but he still retained his impressively large income.

Such a plum position was not good enough for Sergius. In 898 Pope Theodore II died, whereupon Sergius put himself forward for election. As a native Roman nobleman and leading clergyman he was in with a good chance. The Frankish Emperor Lambert, however, wanted a supporter of his named John to be elected. The Emperor prevailed and so John IX took office. Sergius bided his time.

In 904 the papal throne again fell vacant. Sergius decided to try again. This time his luck was in. Count Theophylact was by this time the Imperial representative in Rome and he threw his weight behind his wife's cousin. Sergius was enthroned in the Lateran and settled down to enjoy his time as Bishop of Rome and pope. Count Theophylact was rewarded with the position of Sacri Palatii Vestararius, effectively the prime minister of the secular government of the Papal States. The opportunities for self enrichment were large and Thelophylact grasped them with both hands.

It was as this point that Marozia entered the story. Now aged 15 she moved with her father into the papal court. She was by this point strikingly attractive, well educated and clearly intelligent. Who seduced whom is not recorded but within months Marozia was the mistress of Pope Sergius III. The couple had a son, who was named John. So besotted was Sergius with Marozia that he effectively handed over control of the Papal States to her. Anything she wanted, she got. Egged on by her noble family, Marozia ensured that the best jobs went to friends and relatives of the Tusculum family.

In 909 Marozia married Duke Alberic I of Spoleto. The duchy of Spoleto was one of the richest in the Papal States. Alberic's family had established themselves as self-governing dukes within the Papal States, a status to which many families aspired. With Alberic, Marozia had a second son, also named Alberic. Sergius died in 911, but Marozia did not lose her grip on power. The next pope was Anastasius III, a relative of hers who seems to have been entirely in her power.

Anastasius granted Marozia the titles of Senatrix and Patricia, the female

SERGIVS·III·PP·ROMANVS

Left Pope Sergius III. Pope Sergius III (c. 860 – 14 April 911) was Pope from 29 January 904 to his death in 911. He was pope during a period of feudal violence and disorder in central Italy, when warring aristocratic factions sought to use the material and military resources of the Papacy. Because Sergius III had reputedly ordered the murder of his two immediate predecessors, Leo V and Christopher, and was the only pope to have allegedly fathered an illegitimate son who later became pope (John XI), his pontificate has been variously described as "dismal and disgraceful", and "efficient and ruthless".[3]

versions of the titles Senator and Patrician that had survived from the glory days of ancient Rome. Quite what these titles signified is not entirely clear, but the Senators seem to have ruled the city of Rome while the Patrician was a high official in the government of the Papal States. Certainly the acquisition of the titles secured Marozia's grip on power. She was now effectively dictator of the Papal States.

Anastasius died in 913 to be replaced by a man named Lando. This Lando was not a relative of Marozia's, but he was a friend of her father's. He too did as he was told. Not that he had much time to do much for he died after only seven months in office. Next into the papal chair, and into Marozia's bed, was Pope John X. Another nobleman of the Papal States, John was chosen not for any religious reasons but because he was a good soldier. Together with Theophylact and Alberic I of Spoleto, John put together an armed alliance of Italian rulers to fight the Moslems of North Africa who were raiding extensively along the coasts of Italy. In 915 Pope John X led the combined armies into action and delivered a crushing defeat on the Moslems on the banks of the Garigliano River. The Moslems were never again a serious threat to Italy.

At what point John became Marozia's lover is unclear, but for years he was entirely in her control. Anyone who wanted a Church office or benefice had to go to Marozia. Predictably she favoured those who were her friends or relative, or who paid a substantial bribe. It was Marozia who controlled the curia, ran the government and kept the treasury. By 920 she was the effective ruler of Rome and the Papal States. Her husband Alberic I of Spoleto having died, she remarried in 924 Marquis Guy of Tuscany. If anything is a tribute to the remarkable Marozia it was the way that Marquis Guy, one of the most powerful men in Italy, fell immediately totally under the power of his new wife. He eulogised her beauty and intelligence to anyone who would listen and did whatever she wanted.

However, John turned against Marozia, perhaps because she abandoned him for Marquis Guy. He began plotting with Italian nobles who had not fallen for Marozia's charms or bribes in an effort to make himself master in his own house and take over the government of the Papal States. He even sent an envoy to the ferocious pagan warriors, the Magyars, north of the Alps to see if they could be hired to come to Italy as a mercenaries loyal to the Pope. The effort was doomed to failure.

Marozia was no fool and before long she found out about John X's efforts at intrigue. She and Marquis Guy marched into Rome at the head of a small army. They made straight for the Lateran, burst into the palace and cut down the few men who tried to stop them. They found John and his brother Peter in the papal private office. Guy cut down Peter with a sword, while Marozia seized Pope John and hurled him to the floor for a kicking. The battered Pope was then dragged down to the city prison. A few days later he was encouraged

Below: Pope John XI. Pope John XI (Latin: Ioannes XI; 910 – December 935) was Pope from March 931 (at the age of 20) to his death in December 935.

to sign a document of abdication. A few weeks later he was dead, apparently smothered by the soldiers of Marozia.

Marozia then installed as pope a nonentity named Leo VI who devoted himself to safe prayer while allowing Marozia to run the papacy and the Papal States. Somewhat inconveniently Leo died seven months later, so Marozia told the clergy of Rome that she wanted Stephen, Priest of Santa Anastasia to be Pope, whereupon they dutifully made him Pope Stephen VII. This Stephen was a very old man, which suited Marozia perfectly. She had her own plans for the papacy that did not include having anyone on the papal throne for very long. A few weeks after Stephen became pope, Marozia's husband Marquis Guy of Tuscany died.

Pope Stephen VII died in February 931. Marozia now put her plan into action. John, her son by Sergius III, was now aged 21 and serving as priest of Santa Maria in Trastevere. She let it be known that she wanted him to be the next pope. He was duly elected as John XI.

Meanwhile, Hugh of Arles, the brother of Marquis Guy and therefore brother in law of Marozia, had been elected to be King of Italy. The title was not as grand as it sounded for most Italian nobles were effectively independent, but it did take with it extensive estates, great prestige and enormous wealth. Marozia rather fancied the idea of being a queen so she made a move on King Hugh. The fact that Hugh was already married does not seem to have worried Marozia unduly. Certainly it did not bother King Hugh. He found some spurious grounds to declare that his marriage had been invalid, which Pope John XI took seriously and so pronounced the marriage annulled. The fact that under Church law a man was forbidden to marry his sister in law was also brushed aside by means of a special dispensation by John XI.

King Hugh marched in splendour to Rome to celebrate his marriage to Marozia. The ruler of most of northern Italy was being married to the ruler of most of central Italy. The festivities were magnificent.

The evening after the wedding King Hugh and Queen Marozia threw a great banquet to which were invited the nobles of Rome and much of Italy. At one point Duke Alberic II of Spoleto, Marozia's son by her first husband, came forward to pay his respects. Exactly what happened next is unclear. There had certainly been a lot of drinking going on but it is not certain either Alberic or Hugh were drunk. What is certain is that Hugh insulted Alberic and then went on to make some comments that Alberic and others took to mean that he and Marozia were planning to carve up Italy between themselves. Alarmed for their power and their lives several noblemen followed Alberic when he slipped out of the party. They mustered their men while Alberic ran off to spread rumours among the mob outside that Hugh's north Italian troops were about to be let loose on Rome to pillage, loot and rape. The angry mob stormed the party, led by the troops the worried nobles had to hand. Blood flowed, men died and Hugh leapt out of a window to run off into the darkness. He stole a horse and fled the city. Marozia was left helpless.

Alberic bundled his mother into a private room. He told her bluntly that her days of power were over. She was sent to live in a luxurious villa out in the country, but one that was firmly guarded by Alberic's soldiers from Spoleto. She died in 936.

Marozia had had a spectacular career by any standards. If no woman ever became pope, as would seem to be the case, then Marozia certainly ran the papacy as if she were pope. If anyone deserves to be called the Female Pope it is she.

But Marozia's influence on the papacy was not over. Her son John XI remained pope to 936. But that was not all. Her grandson, son of Alberic II became Pope John XII. Another grandson by Alberic's younger brother David became Pope Benedict VII. Two of her great grandsons also became popes as John XIX and Benedict VIII while a great great grandson became Pope Benedict IX.

Another great great grandson was Peter, Duke of the Column who gained his rather unusual title from a notable landmark on his estates. He was the founder of the Colonna family who established themselves as among the richest and most powerful noble families in the Papal States. The Colonna later acquired the title Prince of Stigliano, which they still hold. Another branch of Marozia's family took the name Boboni. That line died out in the 1080s but not before they had married into the Orsini. The Orsini, like the Colonna, became one of the most enduringly powerful and wealthy families in Italy. They provided at least 34 cardinals and three popes to the Church - the most recent Orsini pope being Benedict XIII in the 1720s. Like their great rivals the Colonna, the Orsini later gained a princely title that they still hold.

It was, of course, the Orsini Pope Nicholas III who is suspected to have arranged the murder of Martin of Troppau who wrote the fullest account of the female pope. Clearly Martin got a lot of his details wrong. But perhaps he was close enough to the truth to worry the Orsini.

Left: The wedding of King Hugh of Italy to Marozia, as imagined in a 19th century engraving. Marozia, born Maria and also known as Mariuccia or Mariozza (c. 890 – 937), was a Roman noblewoman who was the alleged mistress of Pope Sergius III and was given the unprecedented titles senatrix ("senatoress") and patricia of Rome by Pope John X.

About the Author

Oliver Hayes is a freelance writer of books on a variety of subjects. He has been writing books for some years and has had more than 150 titles published in 30 different languages. Some of those books have been for grown ups, but others have been for children aged 5 upwards. He has also presented TV shows and performed on radio as well.

Oliver has written more than a hundred history books for adults and for children. His works show a great attention to detail and frequently take a new and refreshing look at the subjects in hand. He is able to provide artwork references and to check artwork for accuracy. He is also able to produce maps and very often photos as well.

Printed in Poland
by Amazon Fulfillment
Poland Sp. z o.o., Wrocław